わたしが しょんぼりするとき
When I Am Gloomy

サム・スゴルスキー
イラスト：ダーリヤ・スミスロワ

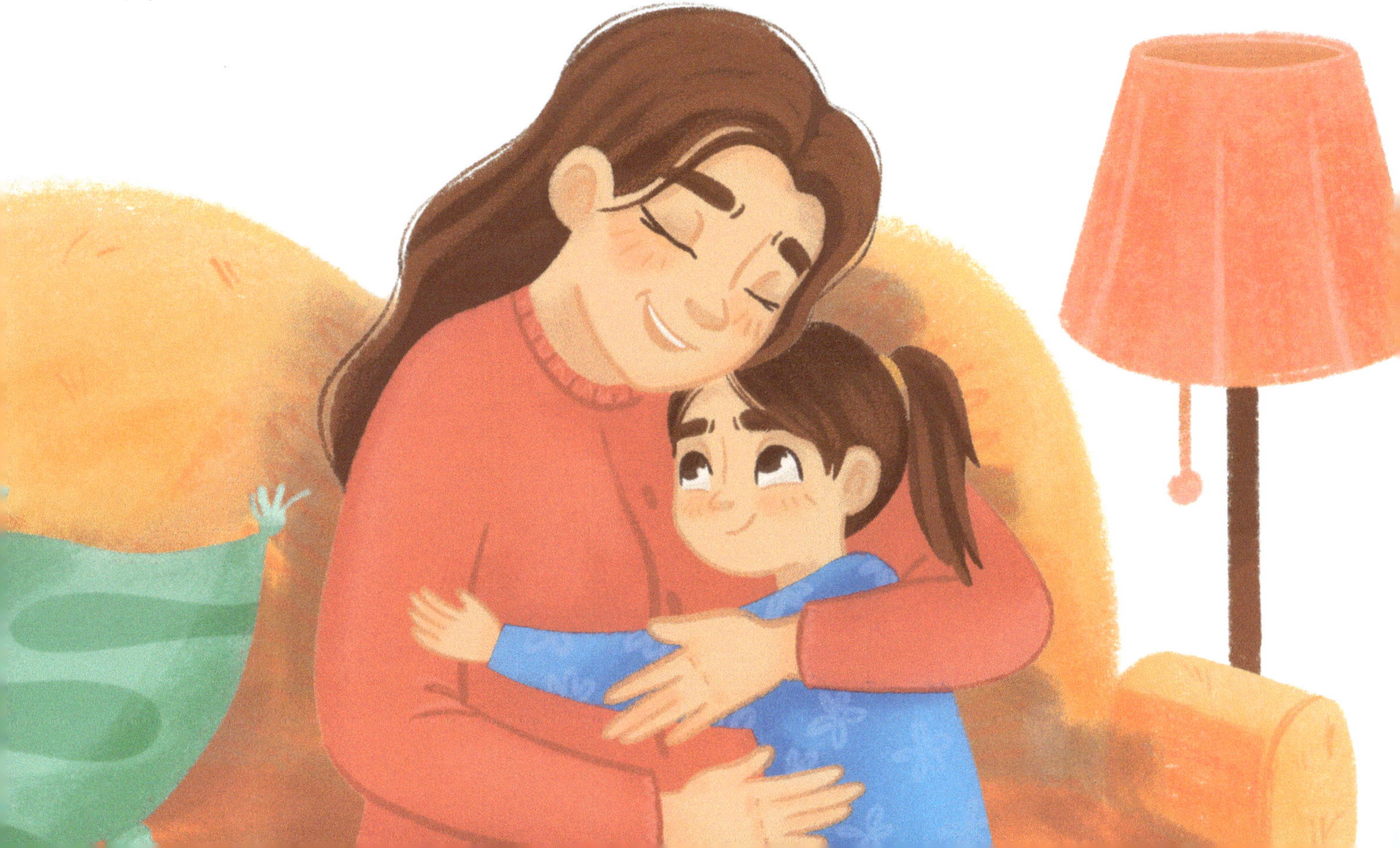

www.kidkiddos.com
Copyright ©2025 by KidKiddos Books Ltd.
support@kidkiddos.com

All rights reserved. No part of this book may be reproduced in any form or by any electronic or mechanical means, including information storage and retrieval systems, without written permission from the publisher, except in the case of a reviewer, who may quote brief passages embodied in critical articles or in a review.
First edition, 2025

Translated from English by Rina Hirai
翻訳：平井里奈

Library and Archives Canada Cataloguing in Publication
When I Am Gloomy (Japanese English Bilingual edition)/Shelley Admont
ISBN: 978-1-0497-0067-0 paperback
ISBN: 978-1-0497-0068-7 hardcover
ISBN: 978-1-0497-0069-4 eBook

Please note that the Japanese and English versions of the story have been written to be as close as possible. However, in some cases they differ in order to accommodate nuances and fluidity of each language.

あるくもりのあさ、わたしはしょんぼりしたきもちでめをさましました。
One cloudy morning, I woke up feeling gloomy.

ベッドからでると、おきにいりのブランケットにくるまって、リビングへあるいていきました。
I got out of bed, wrapped myself in my favorite blanket, and walked into the living room.

「ママ！」わたしはよびました。「きもちがしょんぼりしてるの。」
"Mommy!" I called. "I'm in a bad mood."

ママは、ほんからかおをあげました。「しょんぼり？どうして？」とたずねました。
Mom looked up from her book. "Bad? Why do you say that, darling?" she asked.

「みて！わたしのかお！」わたしは、じぶんのしかめっつらをゆびさしながらいいました。ママはやさしくほほえみました。
"Look at my face!" I said, pointing to my furrowed brows. Mom smiled gently.

「きょうはしあわせなおかおじゃない。」わたしは、ぼそぼそといいました。「わたしがしょんぼりしてても、ママはわたしのことすき？」
"I don't have a happy face today," I mumbled. "Do you still love me when I'm gloomy?"

「もちろんだよ！」ママはいいました。「あなたがしょんぼりしてるとき、ママはあなたのそばにいて、ぎゅーってして、げんきをあげたいよ。」

"Of course I do," Mom said. "When you're gloomy, I want to be close to you, give you a big hug, and cheer you up."

ちょっとげんきがでたけど、それはほんのいっしゅんだった。だって、ほかのいろいろなきもちのことをかんがえはじめちゃったから。

That made me feel a little better, but only for a second, because then I started thinking about all my other moods.

「そしたら…わたしがおこっているときも、わたしのことすき？」
"So... do you still love me when I'm angry?"

ママはまたわらって、「もちろんだよ！」といいました。
Mom smiled again. "Of course I do!"

「ほんとうに？」
わたしはうでをく
みながらききました。
"Are you sure?"
I asked, crossing
my arms.

「あなたがおこっているときでも、わたしはあなたのママだよ。そして、いつもとおなじようにあなたがだいすきだよ。」

"Even when you're mad, I'm still your mom. And I love you just the same."

わたしは、おおきくいきをすいました。
「じゃあわたしがはずかしがりやのときは？」とささやきました。
I took a big breath. "What about when I'm shy?" I whispered.

「はずかしがりやのときも、だいすきだよ。」とママはいいました。「おぼえてる？あたらしいきんじょのひととはなしたくなくて、ママのうしろにかくれてたでしょう？」

"I love you when you're shy too," she said. "Remember when you hid behind me and didn't want to talk to the new neighbor?"

わたしはうなずきました。そのときのことはよくおぼえていました。

I nodded. I remembered it well.

「それから、あなたはこんにちはっていって、あたらしいおともだちができたね。ママはとってもほこりにおもったよ。」
"And then you said hello and made a new friend. I was so proud of you."

「わたしがたくさんしつもんしても、わたしのことすき？」わたしはつづけました。
"Do you still love me when I ask too many questions?"
I continued.

「いまみたいに、たくさんのしつもんをするとね、ママはあなたがまいにちすこしずつかしこく、つよくなっていくのをみられるんだよ。」とママはこたえました。
「もちろん、ママはいつだってあなたのことがだいすきだよ。」
"When you ask a lot of questions, like now, I get to watch you learn new things that make you smarter and stronger every day," Mom answered. "And yes, I still love you."

「もしわたしがぜんぜんおはなししたくないときはどうするの？」と、わたしはたずねつづけました。
"What if I don't feel like talking at all?" I continued asking.

「こっちにおいで。」とママがいいました。
わたしはママのひざにのり、かたにもたれました。
"Come here," she said. I climbed into her lap and rested my head on her shoulder.

「おはなししたくなくて、ただしずかにしていたいときはね、そうぞうりょくをつかってごらん。ママは、あなたがなにかをつくりだすのをみるのがだいすきなんだ。」とママはこたえました。
"When you don't feel like talking and just want to be quiet, you start using your imagination. I love seeing what you create," Mom answered.

「しずかなあなたもだいすきだよ。」ママはみみもとで、ささやきました。
Then she whispered in my ear, "I love you when you're quiet too."

「でも、わたしがこわがっているときは、わたしのことすき？」
わたしはたずねました。
"But do you still love me when I'm afraid?" I asked.

「いつもすきだよ。」ママはいいました。「あなたがこわがっているとき、モンスターがベッドのしたやクローゼットにいないか、たしかめるよ。」
"Always," said Mom. "When you're scared, I help you check that there are no monsters under the bed or in the closet."

ママはわたしのおでこにキスをしました。「あなたはとってもゆうきがある、わたしのかわいいこよ。」
She kissed me on the forehead. "You are so brave, my sweetheart."

「それから、つかれたときはね」とママはやさしくいいました。「ブランケットをかけて、テディベアをもってきて、わたしたちのとくべつなうたをうたってあげるよ。」

"And when you're tired," she added softly, "I cover you with your blanket, bring you your teddy bear, and sing you our special song."

「もしげんきがありあまっていたら？」と、わたしはとびおきて、ききました。
"What if I have too much energy?" I asked, jumping to my feet.

ママはわらいました。「げんきいっぱいのときは、いっしょにじてんしゃにのったり、なわとびをしたり、そとではしったりするんだよ。そういうことをあなたとするのが、ママはだいすきなんだ！」
She laughed. "When you're full of energy, we go biking, skip rope, or run around outside together. I love doing all those things with you!"

「ブロッコリーをたべたくないときも、わたしのことすき？」
わたしはしたをぺろっとだしました。

"But do you love me when I don't want to eat broccoli?"
I stuck out my tongue.

ママはくすくすわらいました。「あのときブロッコリーをマックスにこっそりあげたでしょ？マックスはとってもよろこんでいたよ。」

Mom chuckled. "Like that time you slipped your broccoli to Max? He liked it a lot."

「みてたの？」とわたしはたずねました。
"You saw that?" I asked.

「もちろんみてたよ。それでもママはいつだって、あなたのことがだいすきだよ。」
"Of course I did. And I still love you, even then."

わたしはすこしかんがえて、さいごのしつもんをしました。
I thought for a moment, then asked one last question:

「ねぇママ、もしわたしがしょんぼりしているときや、おこっているときもだいすきなら…わたしがうれしいときも、だいすき？」
"Mommy, if you love me when I'm gloomy or mad… do you still love me when I'm happy?"

「まあ、かわいいこ。」とママはまたぎゅっとだきしめながら、いいました。
「あなたがうれしいときは、ママもうれしいんだよ。」
"Oh, sweetheart," she said, hugging me again, "when you're happy, I'm happy too."

ママはわたしのおでこにキスをして、「あなたがうれしいときも、かなしいときも、おこっているときも、はずかしがっているときも、つかれているときも、ママはあなたのことがだいすきだよ。」
She kissed me on the forehead and added, "I love you when you're happy just as much as I love you when you're sad, or mad, or shy, or tired."

わたしはママにぴったりくっついて、にっこりわらいました。「じゃあ…いつでもわたしのことがだいすきってこと？」とききました。

I snuggled close and smiled. "So… you love me all the time?" I asked.

「いつでも。」とママはいいました。「どんなきもちでも、まいにち、いつもだいすきだよ。」

"All the time," she said. "Every mood, every day, I love you always."

ママのことばをきいて、わたしのこころはあたたかくなりました。
As she spoke, I started feeling something warm in my heart.

そとをみると、くもがながれていくのがみえました。そらがあおくなり、たいようがかおをだしました。
I looked outside and saw the clouds floating away. The sky was turning blue, and the sun came out.

どうやら、きょうはやっぱりすてきないちにちになりそうです。
It looked like it was going to be a beautiful day after all.

www.ingramcontent.com/pod-product-compliance
Lightning Source LLC
LaVergne TN
LVHW072111060526
838200LV00061B/4855